DOUBLE·CROSS MAZES

written, illustrated,
and designed by

Patrick Merrell

Troll

dedicated to:

This edition published in 2002.

Copyright © 1998 by Patrick Merrell.

Published by Troll Communications L.L.C.

Double•Cross Mazes name and logo
are trademarks of Patrick Merrell.

ISBN 0-8167-4820-9

Printed in the United States of America.

10   9   8   7   6   5   4

Helloooooooo,

maze fans everywhere. I'm Avery Waverly, and I'd like to thank you for joining us as we scramble through another exciting installment of *The Wonderful World of Mazes.*

Today, you're in for a real treat! We'll continue our never-ending search for the latest, the greatest, and the unstraightest mazes the world has to offer. Our journey will take us to the far reaches of the globe—and beyond—in search of the little-known...

DOUBLE·CROSS MAZE.

I guarantee that this collection of mazes is unlike anything you have ever seen before. They go not only up, down, left, and right *but also* in, on, by, around, through, over, under, between, across, behind, next to, here, there, and just about any other direction you can think of.

So join us, won't you, as we venture forth in our single-minded pursuit of a first-rate batch of triple-tough, three-dimensional...

DOUBLE·CROSS MAZES.

THIS IS A TEST....

This is only a test. For the next sixteen seconds you will be given a test to see how well you can solve a DOUBLE•CROSS MAZE....

Here is a simple example. As in any maze, you follow paths to try to get from start to finish. The difference with this type of maze is that along the way you go in and out of doors to get to different parts of the maze. All the doors are labeled with letters. Doors with the same letter are connected. For example, if you go in door "D" you will come out the other door marked "D." That's all there is to it. Got it? Then get going!

TUNNEL OF LUCK

We now resume our regularly scheduled program....

Our first stop is the mysterious Seasick Heights Amusement Park. Located just south of New York City, this park is home to one of the most peculiarly tangled rides you're ever likely to see.

Originally named the Tunnel of Love, this ride was soon renamed the Tunnel of Luck because of the confusing jumble of tunnels and waterways that make up its route.

Each Double•Cross Maze works a little differently. In this one you have to travel through tunnels. Beginning at "Start," can you figure out how a swan boat gets to the finish? We have labeled all the tunnel entrances with letters. Entrances with the same letter are connected by a tunnel. Good luck!

And now a word from our sponsor.

3 CRANK-O-MATIC

It slices, it dices, it peels, it grates! It creates perfect julienne fries in mere hours! Just throw in the veggies and crank, crank, crank!

Can you find the path of gears that leads to the big gear at the end? You can travel between gears that touch **or** between gears that are labeled with the same letter. (Gears with the same letter are linked together inside the Crank-O-Matic.)

4 GOING UP

Welcome back. Our next stop is Yonkers, New York, home to the nearly completed Elevator Hall of Fame.

In 1853, Elisha Otis invented the modern elevator in this town. It wasn't the first elevator (the Greek math whiz Archimedes invented one all the way back in 253 B.C.). But it was the first elevator to have a safety brake—a pretty useful thing to have if you don't like looking like a pancake.

As you might expect, the Elevator Hall of Fame is filled with elevators. Each door you see is an elevator that travels up or down *one* floor. Doors with the same letter are connected. Starting at the building's front door, can you find a way to get up to the main exhibit room on the top floor?

5 MAZE BULLETIN

We interrupt this program for an important maze announcement.

You must solve this maze before we can resume our regular programming. Doors labeled with the same letter are connected. Can you get from "Start" to "End"?

6 LINKS

You call it a golf course. Scots call it a links. They should know; they developed the game of golf about 800 years ago from a Roman game called *paganica*. *Golfe* was so popular in 1457 in Scotland that the king banned it so that more time could be given to archery practice.

We learned this while puttering around Edinburgh, Scotland— home of the first formal golf club (the kind you join, not the kind you swing). While we were there, we also discovered a local miniature golf links with a very interesting ninth hole.

To get to the cup with the flag, you have to use some of the other holes around the course. Knock your ball in any of these holes, and it will travel through an underground tube until it pops back up onto the course. You must then strike your ball again from that spot. (Holes with the same letter are connected.)

Starting at the tee, can you find a way to putt your ball to the flag?

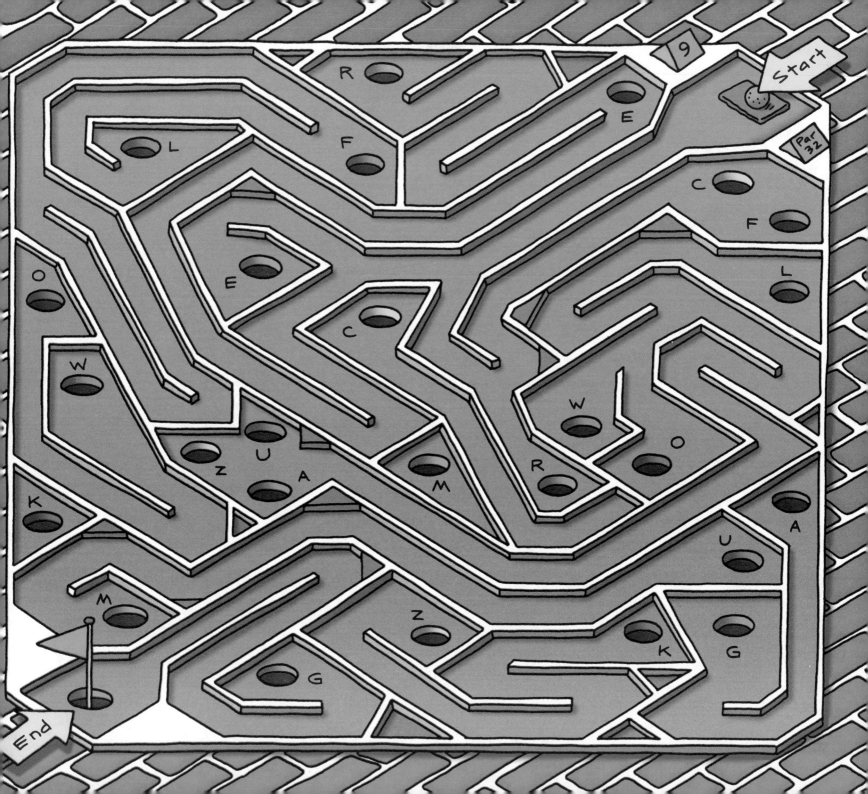

PLANET HOPPING

In a *Wonderful World of Mazes* exclusive, we have obtained a top-secret report of a sighting made last year at an observatory in Australia. The report tells of the discovery of an ancient alien civilization located in a galaxy more than eight million light-years from Earth. (A light-year is the distance it takes light to travel in a year. Guess that ancient civilization wasn't exactly right next door.)

There were no active signs of life, but scientists were able to identify the remains of a complex transportation system between the galaxy's planets.

Here's how it works. Planets are labeled with large numbers. On each planet there is a transport pyramid with two small numbers. These two numbers tell you which two planets you can transport to.

By transporting yourself from planet to planet, can you get to Planet 1?

FOUNTAIN OF EWES

The Fontana Pecore (or Fountain of Ewes) is a monument to the local sheep herders of Bababa, Italy. It has rarely been seen by outsiders. On the next two pages you will see it displayed in all its splendor.

As you can see, the fountain is actually a maze. To solve it, begin on the left page at "Start." Follow the flow of water. When you get to a basin that has no overflowing water, you'll need to switch to the back of the fountain on the right page. Follow the piping to get to another basin. (A pumping system allows water to flow up the pipes—the arrows show which way.) Basins are labeled with the names of Italian cities to help you. Going back and forth, can you get to the large basin at the bottom?

Note: A basin on the left side of the left page will lead to a pipe on the right side of the right page.

So, water you wading for? Grab your fountain pen and dive in....

9 HAMSTER HEAVEN

Put the "ham" back in your hamster with Hamster Heaven!

Hamster Heaven's jumble of tubes and tunnels offers a smorgasbord of fun. Can you find the route the happy hamster at the bottom needs to take to join its pal up at the top? Holes with the same letter are connected to each other.

10 22 LAKES

We've taken our cameras to "the land of thousands of lakes," better known as Finland. There are about 60,000 lakes in this beautiful country. What aren't lakes are forests and swamps. In fact, Finns call their country Suomi, which comes from the Finnish word meaning *swamp*.

Our stop today is a valley in the south of Finland known as 22 Lakes. Local legend has it that, after dark, the mythical "Mad Moose" stalks the forests. To get around at night, the residents of 22 Lakes have equipped their homes with connecting basements. (Houses labeled with the same letter are connected underground.)

Traveling underground between houses with connected basements and boating above ground on the lakes, there is a way to cross the valley without ever stepping foot in the forest.

Starting at the mountain pass, can you find the way to the *finnish*?

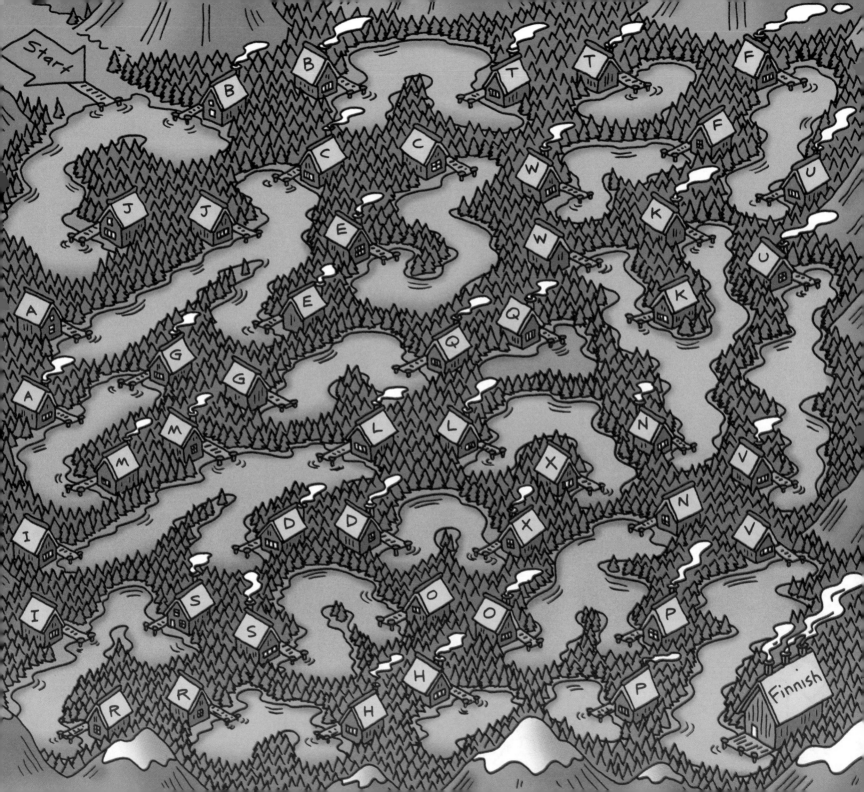

PLEASE STAND BY....

We are experiencing technical difficulties. Please stay tuned as we attempt to repair the problem....

Uh...well, hi there...while repairs are being made...why don't I just...er...uh. Wait, I've just been handed something from our station manager. It appears to be a...a...sort of a maze for your mouth. Wait...I'm being told it's a tongue twister. Very well, then. Can you say it three times quickly?

HOLED IT

Phew...we're back, and this is Abevy Baverby avely grabeling. Now, on with our show...

Prairie dogs. Did you know they are rodents? Did you know they are mammals? Did you know there are almost as many rodents in the world as there are all other mammals put together? Well, I didn't either, but that's what it says on this card and...wait, I'm getting buzzed from the control room. The point?

Oh, yes—this prairie-dog maze. We came across it while in the western plains of Canada. It was right after a small flood had hit. Luckily for the prairie dogs, their holes were connected in such a way that they could get from one end of the field to the other without getting their feet wet. We observed the little critters and marked their holes. Holes with the same letter are connected by tunnels.

Without crossing any puddles, can you figure out how to get across the field?

STATION IDENTIFICATION

You are watching *The Wonderful World of Mazes* on the MAZE CHANNEL, cable television's only 23-hour source for mazes.

Before our show resumes, can you solve this quick maze? Holes marked with the same letter are linked. You have one minute.

We didn't have to travel far to find our next maze. It was made right here in our studios by staff electrician Sparky Watts.

When Sparky asked us if he could create a DOUBLE·CROSS MAZE for the show, we decided to humor him. Little did we know that the complicated device on the next page is what he would come up with. Don't worry, you don't need to know anything about electricity. All you need to know is how to follow wires.

Here's how you do it. Pick a switch and follow its wiring to a set of *terminals* (two screw heads). Each set of terminals is attached by wiring inside the box to one other set of terminals. Terminals labeled with the same letter are connected.

By following the trail of wiring and terminals, can you figure out which switch will turn on which light?

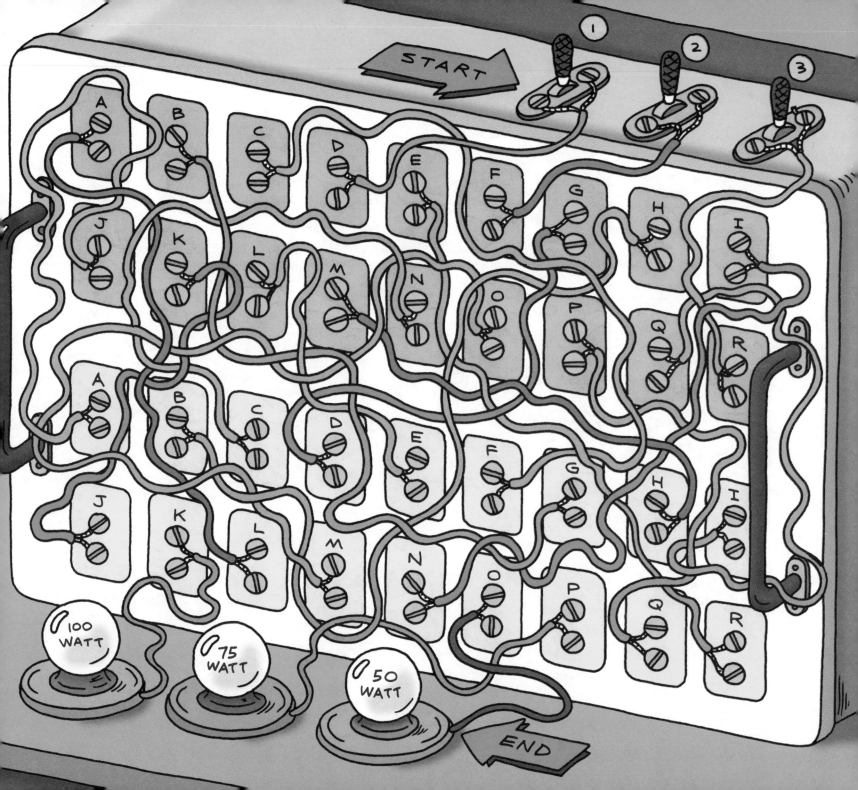

GO BY THE GOBI

In the north of China, separating Manchuria from Inner Mongolia, lie the Great Khingan Mountains. Forests and lush fields are on one side. The hot and barren Gobi Desert sits on the other.

You wouldn't think there would be much reason to travel to the desert side, but there are a few herders and farmers who call it home.

We discovered a way through the mountains using a series of twisting roads and short tunnels. Tunnels labeled with the same letter are connected.

Can you find your way across the Great Khingan Mountains to the Gobi Desert?

NO DRAGGIN'

Indonesia, located between Asia and Australia, is a country made up of more than 3,000 islands. These are the same islands that Columbus was trying to get to when he stumbled across America.

One of these islands is Komodo, home to a nature preserve known as Lizard Land. Lizard Land was built to help protect the Komodo dragon, the world's largest lizard. Just outside the preserve is a large wall that allows visitors to view these 300-lb. (136-kg) lizards.

You will see the wall displayed on the next two pages. On the left page is the entrance to the wall. On the right page is the viewing side. Following the trail of stairs and balconies, can you find the route a visitor would take to get through the wall and back down to the exit?

Note: A door that is on the left side of the left page will be on the right side of the right page. Doorways have been numbered to help you find your way back and forth.

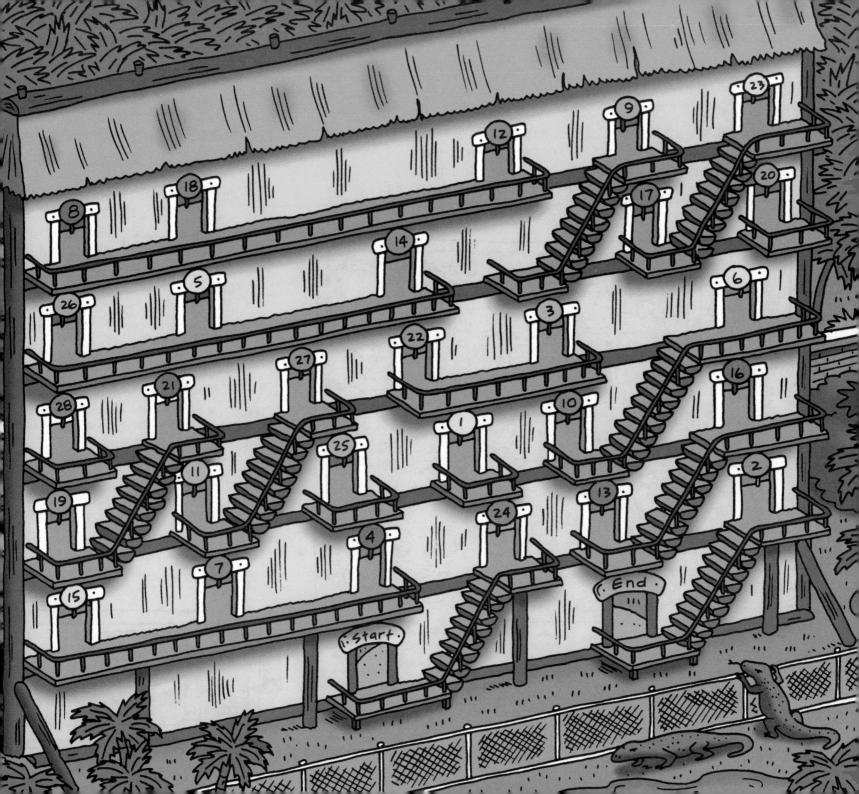

17 WEATHER WARNING

There is a severe weather watch in the area for the next minute....

A storm front is approaching from the west with gale-force winds and raging thunderstorms. You have sixty seconds before the storm arrives to solve this maze. (In this maze you can jump between suns that are labeled with the same letter.)

18 CASTLE HASSLE

We came across our next maze while visiting the beautiful city of Rio de Janeiro, Brazil. Several days before we arrived, a sand-sculpting contest had taken place on Rio's famous Copacabana beach. Most of the sculptures had washed away, but one large sand castle survived and had been taken over by a pair of crabs.

As you will see, these clever crabs managed to dig out some passages through the castle. We have labeled these passages with letters. Passages with the same letter are connected.

Following the paths, stairways, and passages, can you figure out how one of these crabs would get from the drawbridge up to the top?

NEWS UPDATE

This just in from the MAZE CHANNEL's 23-hour news center...

As a result of a study done by our crack maze staff, it has been proven that in moments of desperation, maze solvers have been known to try to solve mazes backward. To address this phenomenon, we have created a backward maze. Instead of starting at "Start," you start at "End" and end at "Start." Got it? I sure hope so. Doors with the same letter are connected.

VILLA THRILLA

Our next maze wouldn't have been possible without the help of an absent-minded gardener named Miguel.

Miguel works at a large villa in Las Palmas, a city in the Canary Islands. One day, as he was returning to the villa, he realized he had forgotten his keys. Because the only way into the villa is through a series of locked garden gates, Miguel had no choice but to dig his way from garden to garden.

Beginning at "Start," can you find the route of holes that got him in? We've numbered the holes to help you—holes with the same number are connected.

Extra credit

If Miguel had remembered his keys, what route of gates could he have taken to get in?

21 SIGN-OFF

And so we come to the end of another episode of *The Wonderful World of Mazes*. I hope you have enjoyed yourself today. I know I have, because it says so right here on these cue cards.

It also says that it's time for me to head home. Just one problem—getting out of this building. The jumbled design of our offices here in the Maze Channel's Maze Complex is so complicated that I sometimes have trouble finding my way out.

As you can see by the arrows, some of the offices in the building are connected. Some aren't. By following the arrows, can you get me from the television studio on the top floor to the street? Thanks.

As you by

Cue #1,642

Cue #1,653

Cue #1,703

It also says t

NEW

FROM THE MAKERS OF THIS BOOK...

THE ANSWERS

ABSOLUTELY FREE*   100% GUARANTEED**   ORIGINAL AND UNABRIDGED***   ACCEPT NO IMITATIONS****

1 **This Is a Test:** D-C-M

2 **Tunnel of Luck:** B-O-A-T-S

3 **Crank-O-Matic:** R-A-P-K

4 **Going Up:** Y-O-N-K-E-R-S-B-L-D-G

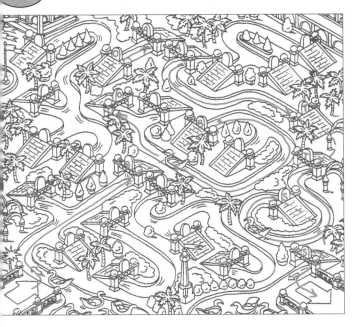

*After purchasing the other 28 pages in this book.
**Guaranteed not to cause warts, except for individuals prone to contracting warts.
***Except for the editing of numerous words, phrases, and sentences that
  made no sense in their original form.
***Unless you really want to.

5 **Maze Bulletin:** X-G-V-L-M-Q-P-Z

6 Links: F-L-A-G

7 Planet Hopping: 2-16-6-11-17-15-10-5-1

8 Fountain of Ewes: Napoli-Messina-Roma-Firenze-Sardinia-Paterno-Salerno-Asti

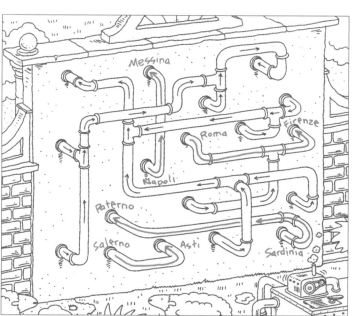

9 Hamster Heaven: R-I-G-H-T-O

10 **22 Lakes:** J-A-M-I-S-O-N-W-F-U-V

 12 **Holed It:** R-O-D-E-N-T-S

 13

Station Identi-fication:
H-O-L-E-S

 14

Switch:
Switch #1:
**D-G-B-H-M-O-
50 watt bulb**
Switch #2:
**F-C-N-I-Q-P-
75 watt bulb**
Switch #3:
**R-E-L-A-J-K-
100 watt bulb**

 15 **Go by the Gobi:**
S-L-U-J-D-N-F-X-T-Z

 16 **No Draggin':** 24-4-15-11-27-14-26-18-12-23-17-22-3-6-10-16-13-2

17 Weather Warning: C-L-O-U-D

18 Castle Hassle: M-J-F-E

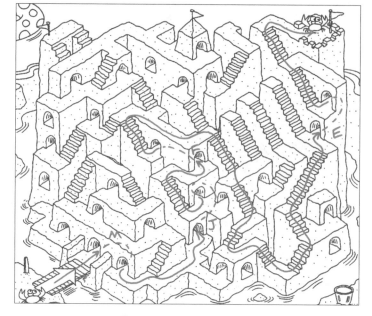

19 News Update: S-E-Z-A-M

20 Villa Thrilla: 6-2-8-15-14-16-20-22-25-29-32-35-36 Extra Credit: blue route

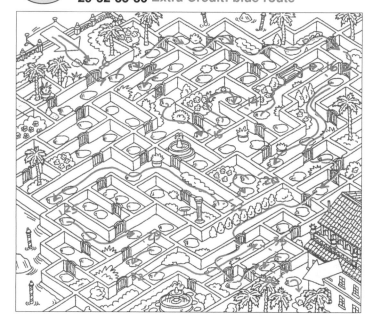

21 Sign-Off: 3-2-10-11-19-20-28-27-35-36-37-38-30-31-39-47-46-45-44-End

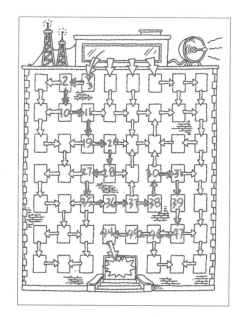

Hello Carolyn and Fieldston !